Look around you
Seaside

Ruth Thomson

Photography by Chris Fairclough

WAYLAND

First published in 2007 by Wayland

Copyright © Wayland 2007

Wayland
338 Euston Road
London NW1 3BH

Wayland Australia
Hachette Children's Books
Level 17/207 Kent Street
Sydney, NSW 2000

Editor: Victoria Brooker
Designer: Elaine Wilkinson
Design concept: Paul Cherrill

The author and publishers would like to thank Chris Jones for help in the making of this book.

British Library Cataloguing in Publicaton Data

Thomson, Ruth
At the seaside. – (Look around you)
     1. Seaside resorts – Juvenile literature 2. City and town life –
     Juvenile literature 3. Human ecology – Juvenile literature
     I. Title
     910.9'146

ISBN 978 0 7502 5145 7

Printed in China

Wayland is a division of Hachette Children's Books.

 Contents

Seaside everywhere 4

Seaside features 6

Things of interest 8

Homes 10

Work 12

Signs of the past 14

Moving around 16

The beach 18

Mapping the seaside 20

A walk along a beach 22

Glossary 24

Index 24

Words in **bold** can be found in the glossary.

Seaside everywhere

The seaside is where land meets the sea. Britain has more than 6,000 miles of rocky, sandy or muddy **coast**.

Twice a day, the sea level rises over the **shore** and then falls again. These movements of the sea are called tides.

▼ Over millions of years, rocks have been finely ground into tiny grains to make sandy beaches. Some sandy beaches are made from tiny pieces of shell.

▲ Some beaches are covered with smooth, rounded pebbles, known as shingle.

▲ When sand is wet the grains stick together and can be shaped.

Harbours shelter boats from wind and rough seas.

LOOK CLOSER!

A cliff is where the edge of a hill reaches the sea. This is a good place to look at the different rocks from which cliffs are formed.

# Seaside features

The **coast** changes slowly all the time. **Waves** batter the cliffs and wear them away. Swirling sea **currents** push sand and shingle along the shore.

Wind picks up dry sand and blows it inland. The sand forms soft, low hills, called dunes.

▲ These rocky stacks were once part of a cliff, but waves have worn them into little islands.

▼ Sea walls protect places from being flooded by strong waves.

▲ Marram grass is often planted on dunes. It stops the sand being blown further inland.

◄ The long roots of marram grass help hold dunes in place.

LOOK CLOSER!

Groynes stop sand or shingle from drifting along the **shore**. Shingle heaps up against the side of the groynes.

Things of interest

All around the **coast**, sea birds swoop overhead, dive into the sea or paddle in wet sand. At low tide, rock pools appear on many beaches. At some resorts, boats take tourists on exciting trips out to sea.

▲ The noisy herring gull is the most common sea bird.

▼ Large numbers of seals gather on sandbanks off the Norfolk coast. Tourists can take boat trips to see them.

This windfarm is just offshore, where there are often strong winds. The thin blades catch wind to make electricity for thousands of homes.

Sea creatures, such as shrimps, sea anemones, shells, crabs and starfish, live in **shallow** rock pools.

Seaweed shelters rock pool animals from the hot sun.

 Homes

Fishermen once lived in small cottages in seaside villages with sheltered harbours. Many of the villages grew into towns in Victorian times, as people started visiting them on holiday by train. Rich people built grand seaside houses called villas.

Today, with less space for building, people often build flats instead.

▲ Each flat in this modern block has big windows and a balcony for people to enjoy a sea view.

▼ Victorians stayed in villas like these for a month or more every summer.

▶ Many old houses are now hotels or guest houses for tourists.

▼ These new houses have replaced warehouses, which once stored goods from overseas.

LOOK CLOSER!

What does the name of this hotel tell you?

HARBOUR VIEW HOTEL
Luxury
BED AND BREAKFAST
Tel: (01983) 852285

 # Work

Fishermen and lifeboat crews work by the sea all year round. In summer, when holidaymakers arrive, all sorts of **stalls** open on the beach.

People have summer jobs keeping the beach clean, renting out deckchairs or working as **lifeguards**.

▲ This fisherman is unloading a catch of fish.

▼ This lifeboat has rescued an injured man from a boat. A helicopter will take him to hospital.

◀ A Punch and Judy show entertains children on the beach.

▶ Cleaners pick up litter that people carelessly drop on the beach.

▶ A shellfish stall sells little pots of local mussels, whelks, prawns and crabmeat.

LOOK CLOSER!

Can you think of any other jobs that people do at the seaside?

Signs of the past

Victorians built long, wide pavements called promenades along the seafront of **resorts**. Some resorts also had a raised walkway over the sea, called a pier.

At **ports**, foreign goods were once stored in warehouses. Now goods are shipped in containers and put onto trucks.

▲ In the past, people strolled along the promenade in their best clothes and rested under shelters like this.

LOOK CLOSER!

In Victorian times, there were amusements, places to eat and a theatre on piers. What can you do on piers today?

14

▲ Small round forts, called Martello towers, were built along the south coast in the early nineteeth century, in case the French attacked. The towers had thick walls and a flat roof with a huge, swivelling gun on top.

► Lighthouses are built on rocky coasts. Their blinking light warns ships to keep well clear.

LOOK CLOSER!

Some warehouses have been turned into cafés or museums. What clues show that this building was once a warehouse?

Moving around

Ships and boats are always coming and going at the seaside.

People sail boats for fun. Fishermen take boats out to sea to catch fish. Ferries take people from one place to another.

▲ Tourists can take speedboat rides.

▲ A harbourmaster directs boats that come in and out of the harbour.

▼ Ferries carry cars as well as people. This ferry goes to the Isle of Wight. Some ferries sail between England and France, Ireland or Sweden.

There are paths for walkers along much of the British **coast**.

Coast Path

LOOK CLOSER!

How many ways of moving around at the seaside can you think of?

Jet-ski

Cliff railway

Passenger ferry

Sailing boat

Inflatable boat

Miniature train

The beach

There is so much to do on a beach. On sandy beaches, you can build sandcastles or sand sculptures. There is often space to throw beach balls and frisbees or play cricket.

People can paddle and swim in the sea. Some like to surf, sail or take a ride on a pedalo.

◀ Pedalo ride

▲ People have fun splashing in **shallow waves**.

LOOK CLOSER!

Why have these rules been made? What might happen if they were ignored? What should you do in an emergency?

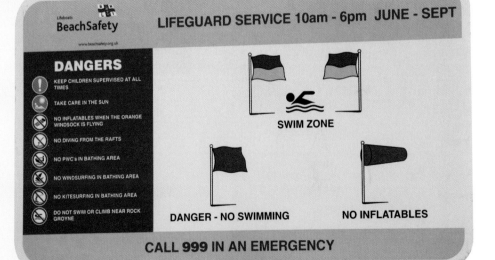

Lifeboats
BeachSafety
www.beachsafety.org.uk

LIFEGUARD SERVICE 10am - 6pm JUNE - SEPT

DANGERS

KEEP CHILDREN SUPERVISED AT ALL TIMES

TAKE CARE IN THE SUN

NO INFLATABLES WHEN THE ORANGE WINDSOCK IS FLYING

NO DIVING FROM THE RAFTS

NO PWC's IN BATHING AREA

NO WINDSURFING IN BATHING AREA

NO KITESURFING IN BATHING AREA

DO NOT SWIM OR CLIMB NEAR ROCK GROYNE

SWIM ZONE

DANGER - NO SWIMMING

NO INFLATABLES

CALL 999 IN AN EMERGENCY

LOOK CLOSER!

Make a list of all the things that this **stall** sells for beach activities.

◀ On some beaches, there are fairground rides, trampolines and donkey rides.

▶ People can buy snacks or ice cream at beach stalls.

Mapping the seaside

Look closely at the map. Notice how:

- the town spreads out behind the whole beach
- a promenade separates the beach from the town centre
- just beyond the town is a country park
- the pier juts out into the sea

▲ Promenade

▲ Harbour

▼ Coastal path

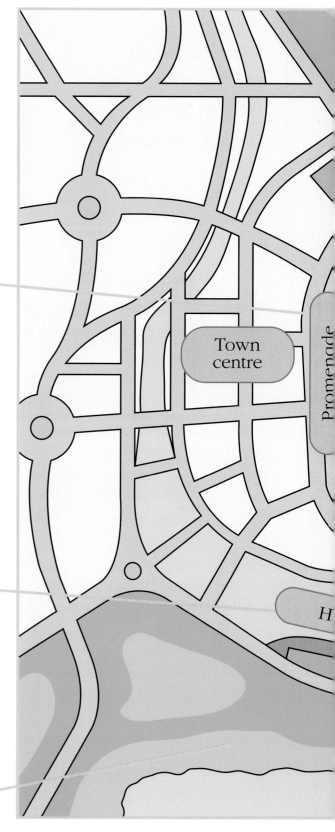

Town centre

Promenade

H

20

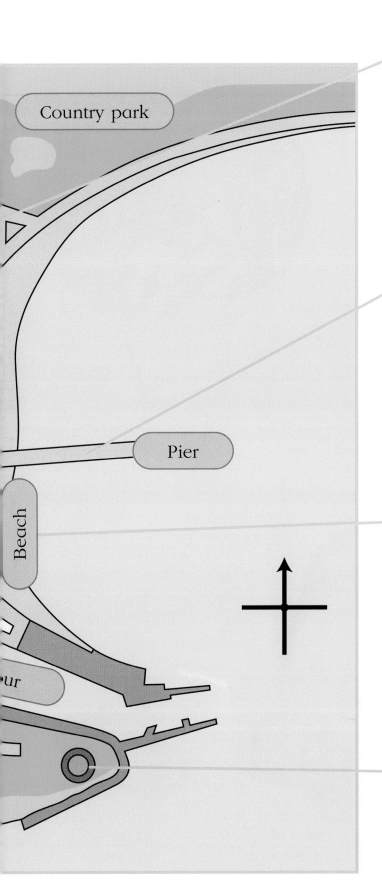

Country park

Pier

Beach

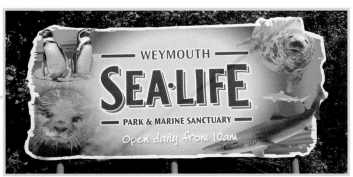

▲ Sealife centre

▲ Pier

▲ Beach

▲ Martello tower

A walk along a beach

The best time for a walk on a beach is when the tide is furthest out.

On sandy beaches, you will often see a line of dead seaweed, shells and driftwood thrown up by the sea at high tide. Look for shells, seaweeds and crabs on rocky **shores**.

▲ Tough, slippery seaweeds can be found on the shore.

◀▼ If you turn over a rock or look carefully among seaweed, you may find a crab hiding underneath.

Driftwood

Cuttlebone (the shell inside a cuttlefish)

Tubes of keel worms

Barnacles on a pebble

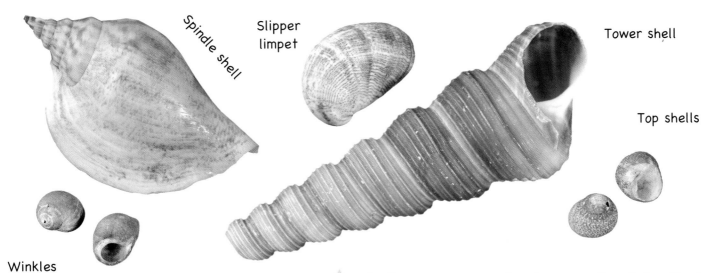

Spindle shell

Slipper limpet

Tower shell

Top shells

Winkles

▲ Shells were once the home of soft-bodied sea creatures called molluscs. Some have only one shell, like these ones above.

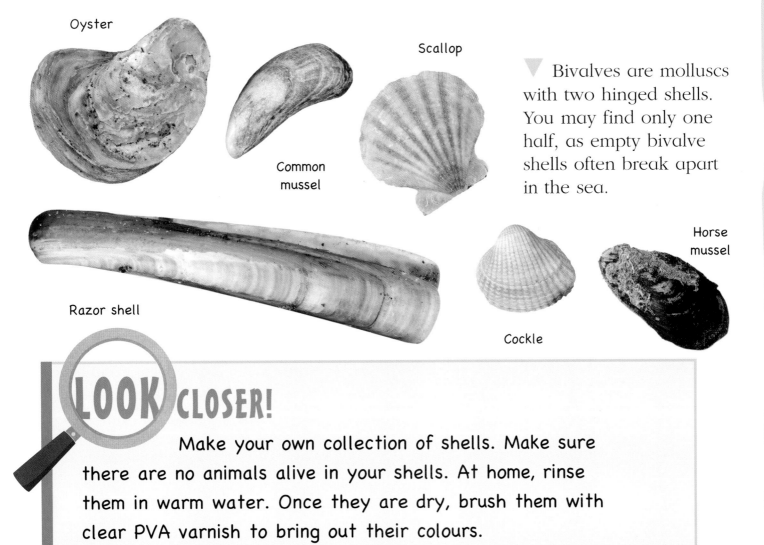

Oyster

Scallop

Common mussel

▼ Bivalves are molluscs with two hinged shells. You may find only one half, as empty bivalve shells often break apart in the sea.

Horse mussel

Razor shell

Cockle

LOOK CLOSER!

Make your own collection of shells. Make sure there are no animals alive in your shells. At home, rinse them in warm water. Once they are dry, brush them with clear PVA varnish to bring out their colours.

Glossary

coast the area of land next to the sea

current a flow of water going in one direction

groyne a wooden or concrete barrier on a beach that stops sand or shingle from drifting

lifeguard someone who works on a beach to rescue people from drowning

port a town with a harbour where ships load and unload their goods

resort a place where people go for their holidays

shallow not deep

shore the strip of land next to the sea covered by tides

stall an open-fronted shop

wave a moving ridge of water in the sea

Index

B

beach 4, 8, 12, 13, 18-19, 20, 21, 22
boats 5, 8, 12, 16, 17

C

cliff 5, 6
coast 4, 6, 8, 17

D

dunes 6, 7

F

fishermen 10, 12, 16

G

groynes 7

H

harbour 5, 10, 20
homes 10-11

L

lifeboat 12
lifeguard 12
lighthouse 15

M

marram grass 7
Martello tower 15

P

pier 14
ports 14

promenade 14, 20
Punch and Judy 13

R

rock pools 8, 9

S

sand 4, 6, 7, 18, 22
sandcastle 4, 18
sea birds 8
sea walls 6
seaweed 9, 22
seals 8
shell 4, 22, 23
shingle 4, 6, 7
shore 4, 7, 22

stacks 6
stalls 12, 13, 19

T

tides 4
train 10, 17

V

Victorian times 10, 14

W

warehouse 11, 14, 15
waves 6, 18
windfarm 9